Christmas Seasonings

101 Quotes and Prayers to Flavor the Holidays

Jean Wise

Christmas Seasonings: 101 Quotes and Prayers to Flavor the Holidays
Copyright © 2016 by Jean Wise

ISBN-13: 978-0-9968688-5-3

Scriptures taken from the Holy Bible, New International Version®, NIV®. Copyright © 1973, 1978, 1984, 2011 by Biblica, Inc.™ Used by permission of Zondervan. All rights reserved worldwide. www.zondervan.com The "NIV" and "New International Version" are trademarks registered in the United States Patent and Trademark Office by Biblica, Inc.™

All rights reserved. No part of this publication may be reproduced, stored in a retrieval system, or transmitted by any means – electronic, mechanical, photographic (photocopying), recording, or otherwise – without prior permission in writing from the author.
Learn more information at: www.healthyspirituality.org

Christmas Seasonings
101 Quotes and Prayers to Flavor the Holidays

Introduction

*The wisdom of the wise, and the experience of ages,
may be preserved by quotation.*
Isaac D'Israeli

I love quotes. The wisdom of concise, inspirational nuggets of truth lifts the spirit and encourages the heart.

Uplifting and thought-provoking quotes around the holiday time brings a sparkle to the season and often a much-needed pause where we stop, rest, and welcome Christmas.

In this book you will find seasonal sayings for Advent, Christmas and the 12 Days after Christmas that will flavor your holidays, add a spirited zest to your life and hopefully give you a touch of the real reason for the season – celebrating Jesus' birth. Advent lasts for 28 days, so 28 Advent quotes appear here. Twelve quotes are designated for the twelve days after December 25 and the rest of the quotes can be sprinkled into any day or celebration throughout the season.

Don't just read these quotes. Share them with a friend. Write them in a card. Take one daily with your morning devotions. Allow the words to refocus your heart and mind on Christ. May their meanings bless your prayers with God.

As a bonus, I have created three bookmarks with quotes that you can download at no cost for you to use and to give to others. Here is the link for these **free** bookmarks: http://healthyspirituality.org/bookmarks

You may also be interested in an Advent devotional book (Barbour, 2014) I wrote several years ago: Let Every Heart Prepare Him Room that is available on Amazon, Barnes and Noble and Christian Book Distributors.

Advent

Advent occurs the four weeks before Christmas and starts on Sunday, four weeks before December 25th. Advent is a time of anticipation and waiting for the gift of Christmas. If we pay attention, God will surprise us with his presence. If we wait in stillness, we will find him in unexpected places, like a manger in Bethlehem.

Advent prepares our hearts for Christmas. Celebrating Advent slows us down to recapture what we are seeking – Emmanuel – God with us.

Advent is a gift. A time to behold the wonders of this expectant time of year. Embracing the themes of hope, joy, and preparation, we hear God clearer in his message of love and salvation in the birth of his son.

Advent invites us to slow down and enjoy the hope and miracle that each day of life brings us. Instead of overeating on carbs we really don't need, we fill our deepest emptiness with God.

We reset our internal watch to God's time. We hear his voice instead of the constant barrage of buy, buy, buy.

Advent reminds us of the lessons in waiting, the joy in anticipation, the pricelessness of hope. Let Advent enrich your soul and open your eyes and heart for the Christ Child.

Advent:

The season of Advent means there is something on the horizon the likes of which we have never seen before ... What is possible is to not see it, to miss it, to turn just as it brushes past you. And you begin to grasp what it was you missed, like Moses in the cleft of the rock, watching God's [back] fade in the distance. So stay. Sit. Linger. Tarry. Ponder. Wait. Behold. Wonder. There will be time enough for running. For rushing. For worrying. For pushing. For now, stay. Wait. Something is on the horizon.
Jan L. Richardson

Advent is a journey towards Bethlehem. May we let ourselves be drawn by the light of God made man.
Pope Francis

This Advent we look to the Wise Men to teach us where to focus our attention. We set our sights on things above, where God is. We draw closer to Jesus... When our Advent journey ends, and we reach the place where Jesus resides in Bethlehem, may we, like the Wise Men, fall on our knees and adore him as our true and only King.
Mark Zimmermann

By his own will Christ was dependent on Mary during Advent: he was absolutely helpless; he could go nowhere but where she chose to take him; he could not speak; her breathing was his breath; his heart beat in the beating of her heart.... In the seasons of our Advent - waking, working, eating, sleeping, being - each breath is a breathing of Christ into the world.
Caryll Houselander

The Lord is coming, always coming. When you have ears to hear and eyes to see, you will recognize him at any moment of your life.
Life is Advent; life is recognizing the coming of the Lord.
Henri Nouwen

Advent is a time of waiting, of expectation, of silence. Waiting for our Lord to be born. A pregnant woman is so happy, so content. She lives in such a garment of silence, and it is as though she were listening to hear the stir of life within her. One always hears that stirring compared to the rustling of a bird in the hand. But the intentness with which one awaits such stirring is like nothing so much as a blanket of silence.
Dorothy Day

What has happened to the old-fashioned, spiritual Christmas? The cause is our disregard of Advent. The church set aside this four-week pre-Christmas season as a time of spiritual preparation for Christ's coming. It is a time of quiet anticipation. If Christ is going to come again into our hearts, there must be repentance. Without repentance, our hearts will be so full of worldly things that there will be 'no room in the inn' for Christ to be born again. ...We have the joy not of celebration. Which is the joy of Christmas, but the joy of anticipation.
John R. Brokhoff

Every year we celebrate the holy season of Advent, O God.. Every year we pray those beautiful prayers of longing and waiting, and sing those lovely songs of hope and promise.
Karl Rahner

Advent—the four-week period that leads up to Christmas—is a series of events designed not to delay the celebration of Christmas, but to enhance it. It's a kind of delayed gratification that culminates in a ... satisfaction that is all the richer for the waiting.
Joan Chittister

In Advent spirituality, we are also called on to meditate on the birthing of Christ in our hearts. In this matter we are dealing with the conversion of life, the movement away from the old life lived under the power of evil to the new life lived in the power of the Holy Spirit. True conversion is a turning from one way of life to another. Christ calls us to be converted to him, to make him the pattern of our lives, to make our living and dying a living and dying in him.
Robert Weber

Advent, like its cousin Lent, is a season for prayer and reformation of our hearts. Since it comes at winter time, fire is a fitting sign to help us celebrate Advent.
If Christ is to come more fully into our lives this Christmas, if God is to become really incarnate for us, then fire will have to be present in our prayer.
Our worship and devotion will have to stoke the kind of fire in our souls that can truly change our hearts.
Ours is a great responsibility not to waste this Advent time.
Edward Hays

You keep us waiting.
You, the God of all time,
Want us to wait.
For the right time in which to discover
Who we are, where we are to go,
Who will be with us, and what we must do.

So thank you ... for the waiting time.
John Bell

Christmas is fast approaching. And now that Christ has aroused our seasonal expectations, he'll soon fulfill them all.
St. Augustine

God is coming! God is coming!
All the element we swim in, this existence,
Echoes ahead the advent.
God is coming! Can't you feel it?
Walter Wangerin, Jr.

Advent: the time to listen for footsteps – you can't hear footsteps when
you're running yourself.
Bill McKibben

A prison cell, in which one waits, hopes…and is completely dependent on the fact that the door of freedom has to be opened from the outside, is not a bad picture of Advent.
Dietrich Bonhoeffer

Take time to be aware that in the very midst of our busy preparations for the celebration of Christ's birth in ancient Bethlehem, Christ is reborn in the Bethlehems of our homes and daily lives. Take time, slow down, be still, be awake to the Divine Mystery that looks so common and so ordinary yet is wondrously present.

An old abbot was fond of saying, 'The devil is always the most active on the highest feast days.'

"The supreme trick of Old Scratch is to have us so busy decorating, preparing food, practicing music and cleaning in preparation for the feast of Christmas that we actually miss the coming of Christ. Hurt feelings, anger, impatience, injured egos—the list of clouds that busyness creates to blind us to the birth can be long, but it is familiar to us all.

Edward Hays

At this Christmas when Christ comes, will He find a warm heart? Mark the season of Advent by loving and serving the others with God's own love and concern."

Mother Teresa

One of the essential paradoxes of Advent: that while we wait for God, we are with God all along, that while we need to be reassured of God's arrival, or the arrival of our homecoming, we are already at home. While we wait, we have to trust, to have faith, but it is God's grace that gives us that faith. As with all spiritual knowledge, two things are

true, and equally true, at once. The mind can't grasp paradox; it is the knowledge of the soul.
Michelle Blake

Sometimes it seems as though we spend our lives waiting. Daydreaming about an upcoming vacation, worrying over a medical test, preparing for the birth of grandchild-our days are filled with anticipation and anxiety over what the future holds. As Christians, we too spend our lives waiting. But we are waiting for something much bigger than a trip, bigger even than retirement or a wedding: We are waiting for the return of Jesus in glory. Advent heightens this sense of waiting, because it marks not only our anticipation of Jesus' final coming, but also our remembrance of his arrival into our world more than 2,000 years ago.
Unknown

*Lord Jesus,
Master of both the light and the darkness,
send your Holy Spirit upon our preparations for Christmas.
We who have so much to do seek quiet spaces to hear your voice each day.
We who are anxious over many things look forward to your coming among us.
We who are blessed in so many ways long for the complete joy of your kingdom.
We whose hearts are heavy seek the joy of your presence.
We are your people, walking in darkness, yet seeking the*

light.
To you we say, "Come, Lord Jesus!"
Amen.
Henri J.M. Nouwen

O Antiphons
Prayed each day at the Magnificat of Evening Prayer from December 17 to December 24. Authors unknown, these prayers are from the ninth century or older

December 17:
O Wisdom, O holy Word of God,
you govern all creation with your strong yet tender care.
Come and show your people the way to salvation.

December 18:
O sacred Lord of ancient Israel,
who showed yourself to Moses in the burning bush,
who gave him the holy law on Sinai mountain:
Come, stretch out your mighty hand to set us free.

December 19:
O Flower of Jesse's stem,
you have been raised up as a sign for all peoples;
kings stand silent in your presence;
the nations bow down in worship before you.
Come, let nothing keep you from coming to our aid.

December 20:
O Key of David, O royal Power of Israel
controlling at your will the gate of heaven:
Come, break down the prison walls of death

for those who dwell in darkness and the shadow of death;
and lead your captive people into freedom.

December 21:
O Radiant Dawn, splendor of eternal light,
sun of justice:
Come, shine on those who dwell in darkness
and the shadow of death.

December 22:
O King of all the nations,
the only joy of every human heart;
O Keystone of the mighty arch of humankind,
Come and save the creature you fashioned from the dust.

December 23:
O Emmanuel, king and lawgiver,
desire of all the nations,
Savior of all people,
Come and set us free, Lord our God.

CHRISTMAS

If you only looked in stores, you might think Christmas starts in August and ends on December 25th at midnight. Some merchants even promote a Christmas in July sale.

Most people celebrate Christmas throughout December while others continue the celebration through early January. Christmas honors the birth of God's son, Jesus.

May the music, worship, cards, twinkling lights, food, and fellowship this time of year deepen your walk with God and refocus your heart to follow our savior, Jesus.

May your Christmas greeting help you know Jesus as you dance in the love of God.

Let your goodness, Lord, appear to us, that we, made in your image, may conform ourselves to it. In our own strength we cannot image your majesty, power and wonder; nor is it fitting for us to try. But your mercy reaches from the heavens, through the clouds, to the earth below. You have come to us as a small child, but you have brought us the greatest of all gifts, the gift of your eternal love. Caress us with your tiny hands, embrace us with your tiny arms, and pierce our hearts with your soft, sweet cries.
Attributed to St. Bernard of Clairvaux

Almighty God, give us grace to cast away the works of darkness and put on the armor of light, now in the time of

this life, in which your Son Jesus Christ came to visit us in great humility; So that, at the last day, when he shall come again in his glorious majesty to judge the living and the dead, we may rise to the life immortal.
The Book of Common Prayer, published in 1662

Give us, O God, the vision which can see Your love in the world in spite of human failure.
Give us the faith to trust Your goodness in spite of our ignorance and weakness.
Give us the knowledge that we may continue to pray with understanding hearts.
And show us what each one of us can do to set forward the coming of the day of universal peace.
-- Frank Borman, Apollo 8 space mission, 1968

Loving God, help us remember the birth of Jesus,
that we may share in the song of the angels,
the gladness of the shepherds,
and worship of the wise men.
Close the door of hate
and open the door of love all over the world.
Let kindness come with every gift and good desires with every greeting.
Deliver us from evil by the blessing which Christ brings,
and teach us to be merry with clear hearts.
May the Christmas morning make us happy to be thy children,

and Christmas evening bring us to our beds with grateful thoughts,
forgiving and forgiven, for Jesus' sake. Amen.
Robert Louis Stevenson

But the angel said to them, "Do not be afraid. I bring you good news that will cause great joy for all the people.
Luke 2: 10

How can God stoop lower than to come and dwell with a poor humble soul? Which is more than if he had said, such a one should dwell with him; for a beggar to live at court is not so much as the king to dwell with him in his cottage.
William Gurnall

<u>Christmas Tree Blessing</u>
Holy Creator of Trees,
bless with your abundant grace
this our Christmas tree as a symbol of joy.
May its evergreen branches be a sign
of your never-fading promises.
May its colorful lights and ornaments call us
to decorate with love our home and our world.
May the gifts that surround this tree

*be symbols of the gifts we have received
from the Tree of Christ's Cross.
Holy Christmas tree within our home,
may Joy and Peace come and nest
in your branches and in our hearts. Amen.
Author Unknown*

*Christmas is a season for kindling the fire for hospitality in
the hall, the genial flame of charity in the heart.
Washington Irving*

*One of the most glorious messes in the world is the mess
created in the living room on Christmas day. Don't clean it
up too quickly.
Andy Rooney*

*Christmas, my child, is love in action.
Every time we love, every time we give, it's Christmas.
Dale Evans*

*Christmas is a season not only of rejoicing but of
reflection.
Winston Churchill*

*The greatest gift you will ever receive will never be found
under a Christmas tree.
It is far too valuable to be stored in any other place
but in the depths of your heart.
Unknown*

*Christmas waves a magic wand over this world,
and behold,
everything is softer and more beautiful.
Norman Vincent Peale*

*Christmas... is not an external event at all,
but a piece of one's home that
one carries in one's heart.
Freya Stark*

*Christmas is a tonic for our souls.
It moves us to think of others rather than of ourselves.
It directs our thoughts to giving.*

B. C. Forbes

*Christmas is not a time nor a season,
but a state of mind.
To cherish peace and goodwill,
to be plenteous in mercy,
is to have the real spirit of Christmas.
Calvin Coolidge*

*Finding the real joy of Christmas comes not in the hurrying
and the scurrying to get more done, nor is it found in the
purchasing of gifts.
We find real joy when we make the Savior the focus of the
season.
Thomas S. Monson*

*Christmas is doing a little something extra for someone.
Charles M. Schulz*

*May you have
The gladness of Christmas
which is hope;
The spirit of Christmas*

which is peace;
The heart of Christmas
which is love.
Ada V. Hendricks

What is Christmas?
It is tenderness for the past,
courage for the present,
hope for the future.
It is a fervent wish
that every cup may
overflow with blessings rich and eternal
And that every path may lead to peace.
Agnes M. Pahro

Christmas —
that magic blanket that wraps itself about us,
that something so intangible that it is like a fragrance.
It may weave a spell of nostalgia.
Christmas may be a day of feasting, or of prayer,
but always it will be a day of remembrance — a day in
which we think of everything we have ever loved.
Augusta E. Rundel

Are you part
of the Inn crowd,

*or one of
the stable few?*
Unknown

---

*Perhaps the best
Yuletide decoration is being
wreathed in smiles.*
Unknown

---

*The magic of Christmas is
not in the presents,
but in his presence.*
Unknown

---

*Three phrases that
sum up Christmas are:
Peace on Earth,
Goodwill to Men, and
Batteries not Included.*
Unknown

---

*Christmas Eve was a night of song that wrapped itself
about you like a shawl. But it warmed more than your
body.*

It warmed your heart... filled it, too, with a melody that would last forever.
Bess Streeter Aldrich

*My idea of Christmas,
whether old-fashioned or modern, is very simple:
loving others.
Come to think of it,
why do we have to wait for Christmas to do that?*
Bob Hope

*It came without ribbons!
It came without tags!
It came without
packages, boxes or bags!
... Then the Grinch
thought of something
he hadn't before!
What if Christmas,"
he thought, "doesn't come from a store.
What if Christmas,
perhaps, means a
little bit more!"*
Dr. Seuss, How the Grinch Stole Christmas

For unto us a child is born.
Isaiah 9: 6

*This season, keep your
eyes and heart open for unexpected ways that
God will reveal to you the
hope of Christmas.*
Jack Countryman

*Our hearts grow tender
with childhood memories
and love of kindred, and
we are better throughout the year for having, in spirit,
become a child again at Christmas-time.*
Laura Ingalls Wilder

*Today in the town of David a Savior has been born to you:
he is Christ the Lord.*
Luke 2: 11

*Christmas in Bethlehem. The ancient dream: a cold, clear
night made brilliant by a glorious star, the smell of incense,
shepherds and wise men falling to their knees in adoration
of the sweet baby, the incarnation of perfect love.*
Lucinda Franks

*Let Christmas not become a thing, merely of merchant's trafficking of tinsel, bell and holly wreath and surface pleasure,
but beneath the childish glamour,
let us find nourishment for soul and mind.
Let us follow kinder ways through our teeming human maze,
and help the age of peace to come
from a dreamer's martyrdom.
Madeline Morse*

*She will give birth to a son, and you are to give him the name Jesus, because he will save his people from their sins.
Matthew 1:21*

*Faith is believing
when common sense
Tells you not to.
Miracle on 34th Street*

*<u>Christmas gift suggestions:</u>
To your enemy, forgiveness.
To an opponent, tolerance.*

To a friend, your heart.
To a customer, service.
To all, charity.
To every child, a good example.
To yourself, respect.
Oren Arnold

Gifts of time and love are surely the basic ingredients of a truly merry Christmas.
Pet Bracken

God came to us because he wanted to join us on the road, to listen to our story, and to help us realize that we are not walking in circles but moving towards the house of peace and joy. This is the great mystery of Christmas that continues to give us comfort and consolation: we are not alone on our journey. The God of love who gave us life sent his only Son to be with us at all times and in all places, so that we never have to feel lost in our struggles but always can trust that he walks with us.

The challenge is to let God be who he wants to be. A part of us clings to our aloneness and does not allow God to touch us where we are most in pain. Often we hide from him precisely those places in ourselves where we feel guilty, ashamed, confused, and lost. Thus we do not give him a chance to be with us where we feel most alone. Christmas is the renewed invitation not to be afraid and to let him-whose love is greater than our own hearts and minds can comprehend-be our companion
Henri Nouwen

Let's approach Christmas with an expectant hush, rather than a last-minute rush.
Anonymous

For outlandish creatures like us, on our way to a heart, a brain, and courage, Bethlehem is not the end of our journey but only the beginning - not home but the place through which we must pass if ever we are to reach home at last.
Frederick Buechner

There were only a few shepherds at the first Bethlehem. The ox and the donkey understood more of the first Christmas than the high priests in Jerusalem.
And it is the same today.
Thomas Merton

I've learned that you can tell a lot about a person by the way he/she handles these three things: a rainy day, lost luggage and tangled Christmas tree lights.
Maya Angelou

Christmas has lost its meaning for us because we have lost the spirit of expectancy. We cannot prepare for an observance. We must prepare for an experience.
Handel Brown

Who can add to Christmas? The perfect motive is that God so loved the world. The perfect gift is that He gave His only Son. The only requirement is to believe in Him. The reward of faith is that you shall have everlasting life.
Corrie Ten Boom

Songs, good feelings, beautiful liturgies, nice presents, big dinners, and sweet words do not make Christmas. Christmas is saying yes to something beyond all emotions and feelings. Christmas is saying yes to a hope based on God's initiative, which has nothing to do with what I think or feel. Christmas is believing that the salvation of the world is God's work and not mine.
Henri Nouwen

Christmas is that moment in time when God, in His unconditional love, stepped out of heaven onto earth, in order that we might one day step out of earth into heaven.
Charles F. Stanley

*One cry awakened the world, one birth changed history,
one life made all the difference.*
Unknown

*We tend to focus our attention at Christmas on the infancy
of Christ.
The greater truth of the holiday is His deity. More
astonishing than a baby in the manger is the truth that this
promised baby is the omnipotent Creator of the heavens
and the earth!*
John F. MacArthur, Jr.

*The Almighty appeared on earth as a helpless human baby,
needing to be fed and changed and taught to talk like any
other child. The more you think about it, the more
staggering it gets. Nothing in fiction is so fantastic as this
truth of the Incarnation.*
J.I. Packer

*He was created of a mother whom He created.
He was carried by hands that He formed.
He cried in the manger in wordless infancy.
He, the Word, without whom all human eloquence is mute.*
Augustine

*Peace on earth will come to stay
When we live Christmas every day.*
Helen Steiner Rice

*Christmas is based on an exchange of gifts, the gift of God
to man – His unspeakable gift of His Son, and the gift of
man to God –
when we present our bodies a living sacrifice.*
Vance Havner

*The greatest and most momentous fact which the history of
the world records is the fact of Christ's birth.*
Charles H. Spurgeon

*Whatever else be lost among the years,
Let us keep Christmas still a shining thing:
Whatever doubts assail us, or what fears,
Let us hold close one day, remembering
Its poignant meaning for the hearts of men.
Let us get back our childlike faith again.*
Grace Noll Crowell

Christmas is built upon a beautiful and intentional paradox; that the birth of the homeless should be celebrated in every home.
G.K. Chesterton

It's sharing your gifts, not purchasing gifts;
It's not wrapping presents,
It's being present and wrapping your arms around the ones you love;
It's not getting Christmas cards out on time.
It's sending any card, anytime, at the right time;
It's not having the biggest and best Christmas light display,
It's displaying the Christ light that comes from your heart;
It's not Santa coming down the chimney,
It's Jesus coming down from heaven,
and giving us the gift of eternal life.
Unknown

Are you willing to stoop down and consider the needs and desires of little children;
to remember the weaknesses and loneliness of people who are growing old;
to stop asking how much your friends love you,
and to ask yourself if you love them enough;
to bear in mind the things

that other people have to bear on their hearts;
to trim your lamp
so that it will give more light and less smoke,
and to carry it in front
so that your shadow will fall behind you;
to make a grave for your ugly thoughts and a garden for
your kindly feelings, with the gate open?
Are you willing to do these things for a day?
Then you are ready to keep Christmas!
Henry Van Dyke

He who has not Christmas in his heart will never find it under a tree.

Roy Smith

Christmas is God deciding to become what He never had been, so that we can become what we never could be. And so, God does the most improbable thing imaginable. He orchestrates His own birth.
Craig D. Lounsbrough

12 days of Christmas

What exactly are the 12 Days of Christmas? This festive time begins with the birth of Jesus, which traditionally is December 25 and continues to Epiphany on January 6th. This period offers us time and space to reflect on what

Jesus' coming as a human means to us and how this impacts how we live each day as Christians.

The Twelve Days of Christmas are also known as Twelfth Night. William Shakespeare's play by the same name was written in 1602 with the intention of being performed as a Twelfth Night event.

In some locations, gifts are given not on December 25, but throughout the 12 days of Christmas or only on Epiphany, modeling the gifts of the Wise men.

May the following twelve quotes be opened as gifts to you, not just now, but throughout the year.

The star of Bethlehem was a star of hope that led the wise men to the fulfillment of their expectations, the success of their expedition. Nothing in this world is more fundamental for success in life than hope, and this star pointed to our only source for true hope: Jesus Christ.
D. James Kennedy

It's true, Christmas can feel like a lot of work,
particularly for mothers.
But when you look back on all the Christmases in your life,
you'll find you've created family tradition
and lasting memories.

*Those memories, good and bad, are really what help to
keep a family together over the long haul.*
Caroline Kennedy

---

*From a theological point of view, Easter is the center of the
Church year;
but Christmas is the most profoundly human feast of faith,
because it allows us to feel
most deeply the humanity of God.
The crib has a unique power to show us
what it means to say that God wished to be "Immanuel"—
"God with us",
a God whom we may address in intimate language,
because he encounters us as a child.*
Pope Benedict XVI

---

*Loving God, help us remember the birth of Jesus,
that we may share in the song of the angels,
the gladness of the shepherds,
and the worship of the wise men.*
Robert Louis Stevenson

*Before we took down the tree each year,
Dad would always say a prayer that we would be together
the next Christmas.*

I cling to that prayer, which serves as a reminder that it's important to be grateful in the present for the people you love because, well, you never know.
Catherine Hicks

Wise men still seek Him
Unknown.

Wouldn't life be worth the living,
Wouldn't dreams be coming true,
If we kept the Christmas spirit,
All the whole year through?
Unknown

May the kindly spirit of Christmas
Spread its radiance far and wide
So all the world may feel the glow
Of this Holy Christmas tide
And then may every heart and home
Continue through the year
To feel the warmth and wonder
Of this season of good cheer
And may it bring us closer
To god and to each other
'Til every stranger is a friend
And every man a brother.
Helen Steiner Rise

*Somehow, not only for Christmas,
but all the long year through,
The joy that you give to others,
Is the joy that comes back to you.
John Greenleaf Whittier*

*I wish we could put up some of the Christmas spirit in jars
and open a jar of it every month.
Harlan Miller*

*I will honor Christmas in my heart,
and try to keep it all the year.
Charles Dickens*

*The only reason I can seek You is the You sought me first.
The only reason I can know You is that You knew me first.
The only reason I can serve You is that You served me first.*

The only reason I can love You is that You loved me first.
You are my reason,
My purpose and my focus in life.
May I always keep my eyes only on You.
You are the reason for this holy season.
Amen
Jean Wise

May you experience God in these words and throughout your life.

If you want to keep in touch and read more of my writing, I invite to visit my blog: healthyspirituality.org.

Don't forget you can download three free quote bookmarks at no cost for you to use and to give to others. Here is the link for these **free** bookmarks: http://healthyspirituality.org/bookmarks

You may also be interested in an Advent devotional book (Barbour, 2014) I wrote several years ago: Let Every Heart Prepare Him Room that is available on Amazon, Barnes and Noble and Christian Book Distributors.

Thank you and Merry Christmas!

Jean Wise is a writer, speaker, retreat leader, and spiritual director. She is a contributor author of devotions for four compilations, as

well as the author of several books, including *Let Every Heart Prepare Him Room, an Advent Devotion* from Barbour Books.

A Deacon at St. Peter's Lutheran Church, she facilitates adult spiritual formation. She has an active spiritual direction practice, including leading group spiritual direction. She is a frequent speaker for gathering and retreats in northwest Ohio.

An RN with her Masters in Nursing, Jean retired from public health in 2006 as the County Health Commissioner to focus on freelance speaking and writing. She discovered her calling to nurture others, as she practiced in nursing, and now as she helps others grow closer to God in her ministry of spiritual direction, writing, and speaking.

Publications:
Let Every Heart Prepare Him Room, an Advent Devotion. Barbour Books, 2014
Daily Comfort for Caregivers contributor. Barbour, 2009
Book Lover's Devotional contributor. Barbour, 2011
365 Encouraging Verses of the Bible contributor. Barbour, 2011
Women of the Bible Devotional and Booklover's Devotional contributor. Barbour, 2015
Whispers - Being with God in Breath Prayers, Healthy Spirituality Publishing, 2016
Spiritual Retreats - Slowing Down to be with God. Healthy Spirituality Publishing, 2016
The Great Communicator – Reflections for Speakers and Writers. Healthy Spirituality Publishing, *2012*
Monthly Musings Journal. Healthy Spirituality Publishing, 2015

Jean has published numerous magazine articles in magazine such as the *Lutheran*, *The Spirit Led Writer*, *Christian Communicator*, and public health journals. She worked as the health and special feature reporter for her local daily newspaper, *The Bryan Times*, for ten years.

She writes two times per week on her blog, HealthySpirituality.org. Established in 2009, the site includes more than 1300 posts. Please check out and subscribe to her blog. She is also a contributor to the Spiritual Directors International blog, to the Northwest Ohio ELCA synod newsletter and is a member of the Advanced Writers and Speakers Association (AWSA).

www.ingramcontent.com/pod-product-compliance
Lightning Source LLC
Chambersburg PA
CBHW041819040426
42452CB00004B/151